Mullett

Quirky, Jerky, Extra Perky

More about Adjectives

To Fiona

—B.P.C.

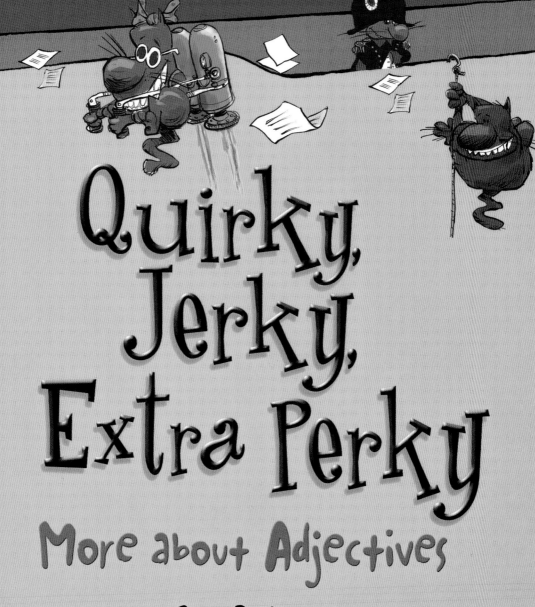

Quirky, Jerky, Extra Perky

More about Adjectives

by Brian P. Cleary

illustrations by Brian Gable

M MILLBROOK PRESS / MINNEAPOLIS

Adjectives are words like yellow, sleepy, slumping, somewhat mellow.

They give us lots of
great description,
like tall, left-handed,
young Egyptian.

5

They paint a picture using words,

like friendly dog

or baby birds,

Spotted, nearly rotted fruit,
peppered eggs,
and leopard suit.

See how these words
tell us more?
A **wild** goat,
a **mild** boar.

Particulars are what you give
each time you use an
adjective.

London's often cool and clammy.

Humid best describes Miami.

Cold's a handy adjective
if Greenland is the place you live.

Like wrinkled hands and

crinkled pliers,

adjectives are modifiers,

telling more about the noun,
like crazy cat or lazy clown.

Kind of **quirky**,

extra **perky**,

quite **polite**,

or slightly **jerky**.

Woolen socks, a knitted shawl—

adjectives describe them all!

Like sly,

sarcastic,

so fantastic,

enthusiastic, and elastic,

adjectives

make phrases sing

and keep our language interesting!

A wilted rose, a chartreuse vase, a cheery, kind, and florid face.

Music that's soothing,
soup that is steaming,
served in a bowl that's
so bright that it's gleaming.

Adjectives tell us
when someone is serious,
fearless or frightened
or even delirious.

Like, "Hear the mysterious bat as it screeches." See how exciting this fun part of speech is?

They modify nouns
in ways that explain
if a movie is brilliant,
bizarre, or inane.

Because we have
adjectives,
we get to pick
words like crumbled and red
when describing
a brick.

or Scary
or splendid,

describing the skating
that Mary or Glen did.

They help us picture
lots of things
when we can't
really see 'em.

Yes, **adjectives**
help make our mind
a kind of **art** museum!

They've told us of a doughnut that was round and plump and sprinkled.

The winking stars above us as they've sparkled and they've twinkled.

28

The sour apple candies
from the cozy corner store.

Adjectives help tell us
about all these things
and more!

So, what is an adjective? Do you know?

ABOUT THE AUTHOR & ILLUSTRATOR

BRIAN P. CLEARY is the author of the best-selling Words Are CATegorical© series, as well as the Math Is CATegorical© and Sounds Like Reading™ series, "Mrs. Riley Bought Five Itchy Aardvarks" and Other Painless Tricks for Memorizing Science Facts, Peanut Butter and Jellyfishes: A Very Silly Alphabet Book, Rainbow Soup: Adventures in Poetry, and Rhyme & PUNishment: Adventures in Wordplay. Mr. Cleary lives in Cleveland, Ohio.

BRIAN GABLE is the illustrator of several Words Are CATegorical© books, as well as the Math Is CATegorical© series. Mr. Gable also works as a political cartoonist for the *Globe and Mail* newspaper in Toronto, Canada.

Millbrook Press
A division of Lerner Publishing Group, Inc.
241 First Avenue North
Minneapolis, MN 55401 U.S.A.

Website address: www.lernerbooks.com

Library of Congress Cataloging-in-Publication Data

Cleary, Brian P., 1959-
  Quirky, jerky, extra perky : more about adjectives / by Brian P. Cleary ;
illustrations by Brian Gable.
        p. cm. — (Words are categorical)
  ISBN-13: 978-0-8225-6709-7 (lib. bdg. : alk. paper)
  ISBN-10: 0-8225-6709-1 (lib. bdg. : alk. paper)
  1. English language—Adjective—Juvenile literature. I. Gable, Brian, 1949-
II. Title. III. Series: Cleary, Brian P., 1959- Words are categorical.
PE1241.C58 2007
428.2—dc22   2006010756

Manufactured in China
4 - LP — 5/15/10